Lucid Dreaming:

an Explorer's Guide

Patricia Smith, MA

CONSCIOUS LIVING MEDIA

CONSCIOUS LIVING ACADEMY | CONSCIOUS LIVING MEDIA | CONSCIOUS LIVING CONFERENCE

For information contact :

https://consciousliving.media

Book and cover design by Aaron C. Yeagle

ISBN : 978-0-578-52846-5

First Edition : June 2019

10 9 8 7 6 5 4 3 2 1

DEDICATION

To my family here and those on the other side.

CONTENTS

ACKNOWLEDGMENTS

There are so many people in my life that have supported me on my journey that I feel I will leave so many people out for lack of space. However, my family and friends have always been my number one supporters and cheerleaders. I should offer a shout-out to my publisher, Conscious Living Media and Aaron C. Yeagle, for giving me the extra push to bring my experience and knowledge to the printed page (or digital page).

My hope is that you will find the concepts and techniques in this book to be helpful on your journey.

GETTING STARTED WITH LUCID DREAMING

DEFINITION OF LUCID DREAMING

The word lucid means mentally clear or conscious awareness in a dream. Achieving the awareness of self and the ability to know you are dreaming while dreaming is the official definition of lucidity. However, there is low lucidity and high lucidity. We want to achieve high lucidity where we can actually control the dream. Not just achieve awareness.

WHY WOULD YOU WANT TO LUCID DREAM?

The subconscious mind has a wealth of knowledge and insight that we can access through our sleep while dreaming. During a Lucid Dream we can consciously communicate with our subconscious mind and direct the dream to find solutions to problems and create faster results of our goals in our waking life.

Lucid dreaming takes time and effort. It is not something most can achieve without dedicated practice. My hope is that these techniques provide a shortcut so that you can achieve Lucid Dreaming consistently.

MY METHOD

I became personally interested in dreams due to a childhood struggle with nightmares that increased during my teens. After trying to find an explanation ranging from various experts suggesting chemical imbalances, too much sugar, repressed trauma and even the possibility of demons, I decided to do some research on my own. A particular psychologist was in communication with a Dr. Stephen Laberge because he had heard that there was a focus on research in dreaming and sleeping disorders at Stanford University. Dr. Stephen Laberge at that time was pursuing a Doctorate and was particularly interested in a unique type of dreaming experience called Lucid Dreaming. The research was showing that this type of dream had many reported benefits including overcoming nightmares.

After personally experiencing several lucid dreams, besides empowering myself to direct the dream plot, I could also access information from a variety of sources within the dream concerning present problems or future concerns. However, I could not figure out how to have the lucid dreaming experience consistently and thus still was plagued from time to time with nightmares and insomnia.

As an adult, I learned about hypnosis and found a correlation between certain brainwave states and the ability to trigger lucid dreaming. I also recognized consistent patterns and symbols that immediately differentiated my dream world from waking reality. My method includes using personal symbols and dream templates to help the brain consistently achieve high lucidity.

PATRICIA SMITH, MA

THE IMPORTANCE OF DREAMS

Do we need to sleep to dream or do we need to dream to sleep? Scientists are finding new evidence that shows dreaming is a necessary part of sleep. As we age we need less sleep and actually spend less time in the REM cycle. This happens around the age of 50 to 60 and often times occur with declining memory. However, there are studies that show that memory can be improved significantly and retained by practice and mental exercises. So, in trying to recall your dreams, whatever the age, it is a good way to keep your brain healthy and sharp.

The subject has come up that we only dream in REM sleep known as Rapid Eye Movement but actually studies have shown that when people are woken during NREM (non-rapid eye movement) periods of sleep they report dreams. The difference is that during REM, our dreams are more vivid and occur more often. Also, we tend to remember the dreams in the REM period because it is the longest of our sleep cycles and is closest to the period of when we wake.

Even though there have been significant studies in dream research, the verdict is divided on how helpful dreams are to people. The best studies were done on war victims who had post -traumatic stress syndrome and had reoccurring dreams of their time in the service. What was significant about the study was that the dreams improved over time even though they were of the same theme. So, while they were still dreaming of the traumatic event, somehow it was less vivid or changed slightly each time they dreamed. As time went by the dreams were less terrifying. In addressing dreams of this nature, the repetitive dreams seem to help us deal with great stress and change our perspective on the past by desensitizing us to the event. Therefore, one most suppose that the repetitive dream is also useful to prepare us to better deal or overcome similar situations if they ever happen again.

It is interesting to note that in animals, while we can only use observation, dreaming occurs with the animal practicing running or a specific task like birds dreaming of their bird calls. So, even while the conscious mind is sleeping the subconscious will be engaged in practice for a specific daily activity. Humans need practice in most anything to achieve better results. In dreams, often times athletes will find they are playing in a game or a surgeon is performing surgery and a student is taking a test at school. This actually may be a way to prepare the emotional state and physical state to achieve mastery over a particular skill. Of course, skeptics conclude it is our daily activities just being regurgitated in dream form. So the actual evidence for this theory is still being debated on just how important our dreams may be to our mental health and wellbeing.

The History of Dreams

It is important to understand though that in history, most dreams were used to receive messages with guidance for future events or present problems and confusing issues. In contrast to today's focus on dreams, psychological benefits for mental and physical health; the dreams focus of the past was less on analyzing the dream and more about spiritual contact with others and obtaining knowledge. This type of dream focus over time became a lost art. Our ancestors always placed importance on dreams. There are countless stories of different cultures around the world having lucid dreaming experiences. The Greeks and the Egyptians had incubating dreams where they pre-programmed their dreams for answers to specific questions. They had priests who would interpret dreams and determine future events for the community.

During the Roman Age, some dreams were submitted to the Roman Senate for analysis and dream interpretation. They were thought to be messages from the gods. Dream interpreters even accompanied military leaders into battles and campaigns.

There are many accounts of people having inspiration through a dream for inventions, or messages that upon waking changed their destiny and the course of mankind. Robert Moss's book, "A History of Dreams" is a wonderful example of how influential dreams have been in shaping everything from our government to important scientific discoveries. Handle's last movement of "The Messiah" was heard in a dream and the whole movement took him only 23 days to compose. The novel Frankenstein was inspired by a nightmare and our periodic table was a product of a dream.

Many dream experts believe that dreams can help in avoiding potential health problems and healing when you are ill or when you are grieving. The Ancient Greeks called these dreams "prodromic" dreams. Research shows that asthma and migraine sufferers have certain types of dreams before an attack. Your bodies are able to communicate to your mind through dreams. The dreams can "tell" you that something is not quite right with your bodies even before any physical symptoms show up. Dreams of this nature may be telling the dreamer that he or she needs to go to the dentist or doctor. If you can understand the language of dreams, your dreams will serve as an invaluable early warning system. They can help inform, advise and heal.

THE RESEARCHERS AND THEIR CONTRIBUTIONS TO OUR UNDERSTANDING OF DREAMS

Dr. Sigmond Freud 1886 – 1939

He felt all dreams were wish fulfillment, repressed urges or desires, sexual in nature. He had limited resources and conducted his research and conclusions primarily from his own dreams.

Carl Jung 1875 – 1961

He felt that there was universal symbols or a collective conscience*. Jung's theory divides the psyche into three parts. The first is the ego, which Jung identifies with the conscious mind. Closely related is the personal unconscious, which includes anything not presently conscious, but can be. The personal unconscious includes both memories that are easily brought to mind and those that have been suppressed for some reason. But it does not include the primal motivating desires and wishes that Freud believed.

*collective unconscious. It has been called a "psychic inheritance." It is the space of our ancestral experiences as a species, a type of knowledge we are all born receiving only unaware of consciously. It shapes our preferences, behaviors and emotions.

Below are some reported experiences that are classified by the collective unconscious:

1.   The experiences of love at first sight, of deja vu (the feeling that you've been here before),
2.   Simultaneous inventions across the world - periods of time where certain themes were in motion during the age. Ex. the renaissance, or the industrial and communication ages.

However, the theory falls short when it comes to dream interpretation because universal symbols change over time. Also one's own perceptions are related to personal judgments based on experiences.

Stephen LaBerge 1967-Present

He compiled a decade of research, received his doctorate in psychophysiology from Stanford University 1980, and is known as the modern researcher of lucid dreaming. He has done countless studies on dreaming and has developed the most widely accepted techniques to achieve Lucid Dreaming.

Mnemonic Induction of Lucid Dreams (MILD) is one of the most popular lucid dreaming techniques, developed by Dr Stephen LaBerge. It involves performing reality checks and setting the intention to have lucid dreams during the day.

Wake Induced Lucid Dreams (WILDs) This is another technique by Stephen LaBerge and involves falling asleep consciously, through the hypnagogic state, straight into a lucid dream. It is more closely connected with astral projection and OBEs.

Yet, some of the greatest minds have disregarded sleep as unnecessary and these great minds did not value dreams.

"Sleep is an acquired habit. Cells don't sleep. Fish swim in the water all night. Even a horse doesn't sleep. A man doesn't need any sleep." --- Thomas Edison, inventor.

"I never use an alarm clock. I can hardly wait until five a.m. In the army I always woke before reveille. I hate sleeping. It wastes time." --- Isaac Asimov, science fiction author.

Thomas Edison and Isaac Asimov both were extremely creative individuals and perhaps they didn't need as much sleep as the average person. The other thought is that maybe they achieved faster REM state. It is highly unlikely they were in a lucid dream state, because a person who has experienced lucid dreaming would definitely enjoy the experience of sleeping without the idea of it being a waste of time.

We also now know that fish do indeed sleep and often times the swimming is an automatic function like our breathing that occurs even while we are sleeping. In studying the great contributors during the age of

Renaissance, it seemed that there was an abundance of genius thought creating many artistic and phenomenal productivity. Yet, the similarity of the people of that age getting less sleep than the average person of today tells me that they were able to achieve a dream state in their waking life or were able to use a cycle of sleep known for short intervals of 4-5 hours. This type of sleep pattern is known at the Phasic Sleep Cycle.

SLEEP CYCLES AND LUCID DREAMING

The importance of knowing your sleep cycle can make a huge difference in your ability to lucid dream and productive dream recall. The benefits of having your optimal sleep cycle include waking up refreshed, better memory and less irritability. In fact, according to most dream research the majority of people do not get enough sleep. During my life I had certain times that equated to several years of sleep deprivation. I would survive day to day on less than 6 hours of sleep per night. This phenomenon is common among many college students and hard working professionals but only about 1% of the population have a gene that actually allows them to function on minimum sleep without adverse effects on our health and mental well-being.

Most teenagers and adolescents need about 10 hours of sleep. Many of us have no idea that we are sleep deprived because we prop ourselves up on caffeine and other alternative energy sources. If you have to hit the snooze button several times before getting out of bed or feel unusually groggy in the afternoon and after heavy meals or driving and find that you are falling asleep watching TV during the day or within five minutes of going to sleep at night than you are probably sleep deprived. In fact, you shouldn't even need an alarm clock in the morning if you know your optimum sleep cycle. The average sleep cycle goes through several brain wave states and lasts in intervals of about 90-120 minute intervals. We have 4-5 cycles per night and actually dream at all stages in NREM and REM (rapid eye movement) but most people don't remember because REM is where our dreams are most vivid and is the longest cycle right before we awake.

Dreamers who are awakened right after REM sleep during the night have better recall than dreamers who sleep through the night until morning. This is possibly because they are in the middle of another sleep cycle when the alarm goes off.

Lucid Dreaming occurs during the REM stage of sleep (when there is sleep paralysis), sleepwalking usually occurs in our Slow-Wave state of sleep.

Sleep Paralysis occurs during REM as a defense mechanism so you don't go running around and living out your Lucid Dream. In fact, there are studies of people lacking the Sleep Paralysis mechanism -- a former boyfriend who gutted his girlfriend while acting out a dream of cleaning fish. If you know that you are one of the few people who lack the sleep paralysis mechanism it is advised you avoid learning lucid dreaming because of its active vivid nature.

Some people experience waking up consciously realizing their body is still paralyzed. These are called false awakenings and are very frightening. Scientists feel this is what people experience when they claim alien abductions or the heavy weight on their chest as a demonic entity.

Falling dreams typically occur during the first stage of sleep. Dreams in this stage are often accompanied by muscle spasms of the arms, legs, and the whole body. These sudden contractions are also known as myclonic jerks. When you sometimes have these falling dreams, you may feel your whole body jerk or twitch and actually awaken from the dream. It is thought that this jerking action is part of an arousal mechanism that allows you to wake up quickly and be on the alert to possible threats in the environment.

**Actually, this state is awesome for OBE experiences (out of body), which I will discuss later on.*

THE BEST TIMES TO ATTEMPT LUCID DREAMING

As you have most of your dreams during REM sleep in your later sleep cycles, and REM occurs in ninety-minute intervals, you should consider scheduling an alarm or naturally waking up during the later sleep cycles.

Experiment with these times to see what works best for you:

After four and a half hours of sleep,
After six hours of sleep,
After seven and a half hours of sleep.

I have also found time spent sleeping to be an important variable. It will often be easiest for novices to achieve lucidity if they sleep to excess — more than 9 hours (think Saturday or Sunday mornings) — and then use the snooze button to wake every 10 to 15 minutes for another hour. This juxtaposition of waking and sleep blurs the lines and seems to make the lucid state easier to achieve. I refer to this state as being the GROG STATE! A person can be in this state while trying to keep their eyes open forcing themselves to stay awake. The time of day does not matter.

I would recommend if you have an iPhone to download the application called "sleep cycle."

If you place your phone next to you while sleeping it can recognize your REM time and help you set the ideal pattern for lucid dreaming.

REMEMBERING DREAMS

Five minutes after the end of the dream, half the content is forgotten. After ten minutes, 90% is lost.

Memories are connected with emotions and the more powerful the emotion or experience the easier it is to recall the details of the memory.

The Egyptians felt that the heart was the center of all memories instead of the brain. They felt the brain was useless and threw it out unlike the other organs they preserved during mummification.

Our brains are very different from a tape recorder and will not store every impression or data we have seen and experienced during our daily lives. Instead, the brain constantly scans our environment for recognition of our personal reticulate activators "the red car phenomenon" - purchasing a new car and then seeing the exact color and model everywhere!

Skeptics say our minds just randomly sorts images as we sleep in order to keep our brain functioning efficiently - kind of like a computer doing a defrag each night as we go to bed.

The subconscious mind can work randomly –unless you give it something specific to work on. When you learn how to input questions into your subconscious the right way, it no longer needs to search randomly for things to work on while you sleep Before you can attempt to Lucid Dream you need to be able to remember your dreams. There are several things you can do to help yourself with dream recall.

1. Tell yourself you will remember your dreams every night before bed and make sure you believe that your dreams will have a special message for you. Using this technique will help you more easily recall the dreams.

2. Stay very still in same position when you find that you are waking up - repeat dream in your head

without moving and you will be able to make recall last longer.

3.   Don't use a jarring alarm clock - waking up gently helps with remembering.

4.   Knowing your ideal sleep cycle can also help you wake up where you are at the end of your REM sleep cycle allowing for fresh memories to be written down before entering another cycle.

5.   Use a Dream Journal, keep it by your bed at night. If you have a partner who you are trying to keep from disturbing than I recommend a night pen or going to the bathroom and writing down just the basics of the dream. No need to write down the full narration.

Smell has long been associated as a powerful trigger for memories. I can recommend using aromatherapy inhalers or essential oils before bed and upon waking to encourage better memory of the dreams.

Fish oil also indirectly improves your dream recall because it makes your content more vivid and intense. (Or, as often-reported nightmares can invoke such a powerful emotion that it is imprinted on your memory.)

While we are dreaming our brains tend to pull from long associated memories rather than short-term events and impressions. The language centers are also usually shut off which is why it's much harder to read in a dream. What's more, our perception of time is altered, so that if you're having a vivid dream with a huge sprawling plot sequence, it can feel like you have dreamt for 100 years.

Studies have shown that brain waves are more active when we are dreaming than when we are awake.

DREAMS AND SOUL EVOLUTION

The theory of past lives have converted many skeptics due to regression hypnosis which can tap into the subconscious mind and obtain knowledge or skills that seem to originate from another time in history and life. However, lucid dreams can also tap into this knowledge. Studies have shown that some people will dream and in the dream they are speaking fluently a different language or a special skill like playing the piano and doing complex mathematical equations. Are dreams a way to speed up our spiritual evolution by experiencing different realities and time? If we can acquire these skills by dreaming it doesn't make sense to me why we would need to be reincarnated. Many people have experienced the answers to problems being easily solved by the cliché action of just sleeping on it.

DREAM SEQUENCES

The phenomenon of having a dream sequence is very rare. A Dream sequence is defined as a series of dreams that make up a continual narrative building upon the same background archetypes and storyline. I compare it to a television mini-series without the commercials.

Examples of dream sequences are dreams that continue a storyline from where a former dream stopped. The sequence can be experienced in the same night during a different period of a sleep cycle or on a completely different night. I have had dream sequences that have spanned over years of time. You may find that your dream seems to have a déjà vu feel to you when you are having a dream sequence or you may find the same scenery or even the same characters within a new storyline.

Either way, certain aspects of the dream are always exactly the same and it literally seems to the dreamer as if it is a separate reality. I have heard people say it is the closest thing they can experience to living in a parallel universe.

However, a dream sequence is not the same as what is called the Repetition Principle. The repetition principle can also be a reoccurring dream that seems to have the same plot or characters and scenery. The difference is that the dream sequence has a connected storyline that continues the plot regardless of the amount of time separation when the dreams are occurring.

What is the significance of dream sequences? Our brain prefers familiarity versus the unknown experience. In fact, we usually have a natural aversion to change. Even though it is a cliché, we really are "creatures of habit." Anything that is an unknown is actually perceived as a negative in our brain. I learned this from studying hypnosis and how addictive behaviors are formed at the subconscious level. When we experience a dream sequence or the repetition principle, our subconscious brain is choosing a familiar pattern to use as a way for us to remember the message.

In fact, having a dream sequence or a repeating dream is one of the best ways for us to jump into a lucid dream experience. It is a fantastic trigger to bring the conscious knowledge of awareness while we are dreaming. Through my dream sequence experience, I have perfected a method based on these concepts to have a consistent template the brain can use to create lucid dreams.

**Templates – (I have provided some examples for you to use at the end of this guide.)

As a young child I would consistently have dreams that would start with the same scenario. I was in front of a calm lake in the middle of woodland clearing. Beside me was an already lit oil lamp that had a little carrying handle. I would take the oil lamp in hand and walk into the woods following a path that led me to an old temple in ruins. When I went into the temple I found a stone alter which had tons of paper scrolls rolled up and tied with red velvet ribbons. From there, the dream would take different directions.

Sometimes I would find another person appearing in the temple to take me on an adventure. Other times my dream would involve me taking a scroll and being chased. Most of the time I would take a scroll and start reading what was written in the scroll. The scroll on some occasions would transform itself into a portal to another world. As I got older I found that if I wanted to know a solution to a problem the scroll would often tell me the next step to take or would turn into a movie screen showing me important information. I now use this method in a variety of ways to receive guidance.

Using dream templates in a repetitive fashion help create an accelerated approach to lucid dreaming and establish the architecture and symbols our brains utilize to communicate back to us in a way that is easier for us to access the messages. In my experience, the method induces more dream sequences, which delivers so many benefits. If a person can commit to the initial work entailed to train our brains to utilize the template, we can surprise ourselves with our precognitive abilities. Besides having more intuition and insight, we can gain better awareness during the day and find that our lives are increasingly more fulfilling, synchronistic and less stressful.

There is a method I have heard of called "Quantum Jumping" by Burt Goldman. The theory is based on creating an alternative reality of all the scenarios and achievements you would like to experience by projecting yourself in that role as if it is an alternate reality of yourself. The author of this method states that in doing this consciously you are preparing yourself for the reality to manifest faster and with greater accuracy for our highest good, rather than just our carnal desires.

While I like his method and think it can benefit people in ways like the concepts portrayed in the movie "The Secret;" I believe dreaming is a much more powerful way to accelerate our best life into action. The subconscious holds pre-conceived information we have gathered through our lifetime. These are deeply embedded belief systems we have retained about ourselves and our environment. We allow our conscious mind the power to filter most messages we receive on a daily basis. I like how Dr. Patrick Porter author of "Awaken the Genius" compared our brains to a computer. Our brains operate using a set of rules.

He stated that the conscious mind accounts for an average of 8% of the minds total thinking and processing power. He goes on to say that the awareness of who we are is the function of the conscious mind and the subconscious part which accounts for 92% of stored data is the reality of who we are.

However, unless the subconscious mind receives enough data, which delivers the right belief systems we seek, it will continue to defy the conscious will to change. This is why hypnosis techniques are so helpful in changing a variety of behaviors like nail biting, low self-esteem, lack of motivation, bad habits and improving positive thinking. The hypnotist can literally re-program the subconscious mind to align both brains to achieve dramatic changes. All hypnosis is actually a form of self-hypnosis and we can use similar techniques to gain these benefits during lucid dreaming. The act of consciously dreaming requires dedication of practice and technique much like learning to play an instrument. However, lucid dreaming is a skill anyone can achieve and has a lot of advantages to other personal development methods. By learning this valuable method you can save yourself money and time in the comfort of your own home without anyone knowing while you sleep!

THE LUCID DREAMING PROCESS

The first step in achieving these skills, involve your acute attention to any familiar dream sequences you may have had in the past. These dreams would be a great starting place for building your own unique template. Usually, dream dictionaries depict common universal symbols and their meanings in a way to help analyze our dreams. These are not very useful because our brains are all uniquely different in our perceptions based on our past experiences and cultural constructs or family influences. For example, many people are afraid of snakes but there are also people who love to keep pets as snakes and enjoy these creatures without any fear. The same can be said of people's feelings towards rain, certain colors and even common activities like driving or reading.

I would like you to start with an exercise that determines your positive and negative neuro associations. Our subconscious mind will reject or view an object and event with fear if it is an unknown. This is because we are still initial responders of the fight or flight syndrome when it comes to these associations. I have always wondered why a person would continue to do something they consciously know is bad for them or seem addicted to a behavior that they desperately want to change.

The conscious mind perceives any familiar pattern or experience no matter how negative it is for us as more comforting than the fear of changing into an experience that has unknown results. Therefore, the subconscious mind is continually fighting our will to change preferring the negative familiar to the positive unfamiliar experiences.

In dream analysis the best way to tackle the meanings is to create a dictionary of your own symbolic triggers that create a positive or negative association in your brain. These should only be familiar experiences that you have had. Any unknown objects or events should be addressed in a different section of your notebook.

Create two columns as follows:

Positive: **Negative:**

Under each heading list off the top of your head as many examples of positive symbols and events that instantly bring joy and smile to your face. Under the negative heading list off as many unhappy or scary negative associations that you have experienced.

Here is my example:

Positive:	Negative:
Flowers	Spiders
Chocolate Ice Cream	Math
Puppies	Body Odor
Green	Gyms
Waterfalls	Sharks
Forests	Heights
Sunshine	Swimming
Warm Rain	Ocean
Baths	Noise
Bubbles	Dirty House

Swinging	Clutter
Hiking	Darkness
Kayaking	Tickling
Ice Skating	Performance
Singing	Dentist
Music	Smoke
Piano	Rules
Painting	Time
Pizza	Watches
Mysteries	Planes
Puzzles	Flying
Reading	Wrestlers

These lists should be kept handy and should be several pages long as you build your personal dream guide. You can also add people presently in your life, past and celebrities you would like to meet or dislike. Also, be honest with yourself if you have socially unacceptable likes and dislikes.

Unfortunately, many of us would like to be more open and accepting of people and behaviors but despite what is culturally or politically correct the ideal doesn't change our underlying beliefs based on our former filters we established early in life. During the day try to catch yourself making internal snap judgments as you go about your activities. Also, as you look back at your list of neuro-associations try to write in a brief word labeling the initial feeling you have. For example next to the word "heights" – I put the word "fear" down by it in my notebook. The word "Bubbles" I put the word "carefree." You can couple words into a phrase also if you desire. Make it a snappy quick response and don't spend lots of time questioning why or worry that you have picked the wrong adjective to describe your attitude.

PATRICIA SMITH, MA

KNOW THYSELF BEFORE LUCIDITY

I am providing a few exercises that I feel are important steps before attempting lucid dreaming. The next exercise below involves you asking friends and relatives these questions:

- Are there any words or phrases I say often?
- Do you wonder why I have certain gestures or mannerisms and what are they?
- If you could help me change 3 things that would benefit my life what would they be?
- Are there any dislikes or likes that I have which seem a bit odd to you?

- What is the first sign that I show when I am scared or troubled? How about when I get excited or happy?
- To someone who has slept beside you often⋯ask him or her if you are a sound sleeper or if you talk or move erratically and if so, is it all-night or just in the morning or evening. Do you snore?

It is said by some researchers that when a person is snoring they are not dreaming.

After asking as many of your close friends and family these questions, collect the answers by recording them in your dream guide.

Why are these questions important?

Because our dreams are meant to help us work to a better understanding of ourselves and open our minds up to knowledge and enlightening experiences. We have to start with a self-discovery process that uncovers the way our sub-conscious mind is trying to communicate with us. My good friend Rhonda, who has a thriving counseling practice in Colorado, uses a method she developed called the "Liberator Method."

She treats clients based on the exact words they speak to her when describing their problems. Along with other psychology tools she is able to help them understand that they are literally "speaking" their issues and solutions without conscious awareness. For example, I was telling her in confidence about issues I always seem to have with my car. I was frustrated because for some unknown reason my vehicle seems to break down or have problems, which defy the careful attention I give to servicing and maintaining the car. She was able to ask me certain questions to pinpoint the fact that my car was my vehicle and represented my literal body. She was hearing me speak about being trapped and frustrated that it was not working to my satisfaction. We realized that most of my car problems had been escalating for the past 5 years and it correlated with some health issues I was personally working to treat. I also was having a lot of lucid flying dreams and told her that I used to have a fantasy as a kid that I was a bird and would love to sit up high in a tree and imagine jumping off and flying into the sunset.

Based solely on my literal words we uncovered that as a young child I felt invincible and my body was lithe, lightweight and I was the best at everything physical and athletic. I also had no fears of heights until later in life. My spirit literally wanted to have a body that let it be as free as I felt in my flying dreams and how I felt as a child. The car represents to me my frustrations with my constant need to keep up my body. No matter what I do the fact of my getting older is going to make the upkeep even harder. She felt I was literally manifesting car problems to get my brain to understand and accept that I need to release that desire of perfection and love the body I have knowing I will have a spiritual body that is perfect when I die.

I have taken her theory one step further in that our subconscious minds also have the insight into our future and if we pay careful attention to the literal words we are saying daily, we can use them to speak to our dreaming minds at night!

There is a popular show on TV called "Celebrity Ghost Stories." I find the stories to be very entertaining and one night the late David Carradine was telling a story about a haunting he experienced after moving in with a lady whose husband died a few years earlier. He used words like··· "I guess ghosts just HANG around a lot to check on loved ones." He repeatedly used the word HUNG and HANG over and over as he narrated his story. Then he ended the story saying he found a

TIE that said GRATEFUL DEAD on it and he felt it was a message from the ghost.

Four months later David was found hung from his neck tied up dead in a hotel room. Was he literally speaking the future circumstances of his own death??? Rhonda would probably say yes! Eerie to say the least don't you think? The book "Messages from 9/11," also tells of the survivors having signals and literal words from loved ones prior to their passing. I firmly believe our subconscious mind knows when our time is done on this planet. Not sure if I would want to discover that for myself unless I could prevent it from happening. However, our literal words are our own map in charting the world of lucid dreaming.

PATRICIA SMITH, MA

BELL WORDS

The previous exercise helped you to discover your Bell words and phrases; these are areas you are stuck in or need to express. You will have help or special attention directed to the message. You will also be able to have insight from your specific mannerisms and gestures. You might be surprised to hear that there are stories you tell over and over again. (This is an indication that you are getting a need met by telling this story or perhaps wanting subconsciously to have different perspectives in order to work out a solution.)

I found I was repeating stories and it was a bit weird to hear because I didn't remember consciously telling it so many times. Also, I was saying the word "absolutely" as filler for when I was tuning out a conversation but wanted to appear as if I was listening. I had a friend that constantly twirled her hair when she was nervous and I would always catch my dad subconsciously cutting his hair with his fingers behind his left ear, as he would drive. Every time he did this action I knew my dad would get his hair cut that week because his hair was too long.

The question about knowing your first physical signs of fear and excitement are useful tools to trigger lucidity in dreams and I will explain more in detail a bit later in this book. Finally, knowing if you have talking or sleepwalking issues as you sleep will help to determine if lucid dreaming is right for you. The information is also helpful for determining how light or deep a sleeper you are and points to your optimum sleeping cycle.

NIGHTMARES AND LUCID DREAMING

Night terrors or bad dreams can be extremely upsetting and disruptive to our mental state. We can find ourselves upset for days when we have a terrifying or upsetting dream. As a child I found nightmares to be more prevalent than any other dream and dreaded the bedtime hour.

What does it mean when we have a nightmare? There are many types of nightmares, which involve disturbing images and aspects that upset our emotional state. Usually we find ourselves waking up in a cold sweat or having someone else shake us awake. Nightmares can appear as a warning to us about something we are not dealing with in our daily waking life. They also can come about when there are health issues or chemical and hormonal imbalances in our body.

** The more repetitive these dreams become the more necessary it is to determine the message we need to receive.

Many people find that nightmares are deep seeded fears that are able to play out without harm while we sleep. Nightmares can be very therapeutic because it can show us the worst outcome of our choices or being victimized without it actually harming us. How many times have you woken up and let out a big sigh of relief when you realized the dream was not real? Repressed emotions of anger and fear can express itself as exaggerated terror and rage in the form of a bad dream. In a way, these bad dreams are good for us in allowing our shadow selves to play out scenarios that do not cause actual consequences for our self or others in daily events.

However, experiencing these nightmares can still be just as disturbing and nobody wants to have these dreams as a reoccurring visitor during sleep. The first step to understanding nightmares is to focus on the exact emotion you were experiencing in the dream and the initial point of waking. Sometimes the emotions are different and mixed with other thoughts or feelings. At other times the emotion is overwhelmingly one aspect like fear or anger, helplessness or even pain. Look at the pattern of your nightmares and try to figure if there are always certain themes that are appearing. Mine were always similar to a Scooby Doo episode where a good dream would surprisingly go bad and I would end up having to face someone or something trying to kill me. Blood was always featured and also my dream friend Kaiyen who would come to save the day by giving me some clue, riddle to solve or weapon that would magically fight off the monster or bad person. After many years of enduring these dreams I faced my deepest fears and started to work on being independent. I was very sheltered growing up and being the baby of the family led to a dependence on my parents, which did not add to my confidence of being able to do things on my own. I was a dare devil in many ways and yet absolutely terrified when night approached. If nightmares are reoccurring they are meant to stir you into action and should be heeded as a warning of attention.

Many health problems can begin 6 months prior without any conscious knowledge of symptoms. If a person can heed the warning from the dream, many times the disease or health issue will be avoided.

Usually, if the dream involves your health a body part will be somewhat magnified in a strange way. For example, you will find yourself bald or maybe you look down at your hand and it is covered with a glove or looks rusted. I was once told by a friend that before she was paralyzed she would have frightening dreams that involved her always being carried by someone else or riding on strange animals. One of her dreams even involved her seeing her legs as wheels instead of feet. One of the big questions I always get asked, " if I see or notice a health issue what can I do to prevent it from actually manifesting?" Well, for one, go to your doctor and get a thorough examination of the health issue you are dreaming about. If everything is good than take preventative measures to ensure your safety and make sure you are eating well or exercising etc. I also suggest practicing the art of inserting the opposite of what you are fearing in the "grog state" so upon dreaming, the unconscious can better clarify the message or begin the process of accepting the other reality as the truth which then in turn promotes healing and eliminates the former consequences from playing out in the future.

We can use this same technique for dealing with any underlying fears. Instead of crashing in that plane, create the dream outcome of personal empowerment. This can include you flying the plane, safely landing, or imagining angels accompanying the plane on your journey. Depending on your belief system I have had many people tell me that reoccurring nightmares means you are being oppressed by an outside evil or possibly a demon. In fact while attending a church in college I had prayers to exorcise a demon they thought was plaguing my dreams with nightmares.

After much careful analysis of my dreams I came to the conclusion that the dream character that always appeared in my nightmare was of a dual nature. Sometimes he would save me from the negative experience and other times he seemed to use riddles and have a mischievous nature about him. Still, I would always feel somehow enlightened by the experience even if it was stressful. While I have no idea if there is truth to having demons appear in our dreams, I do believe there is powerful sometimes-spiritual forces at work and some of those forces are negative in nature. One time I had a very negative experience sleeping in a hotel when I was working at a dinner theatre during a summer in college. The owners had informed us when we came to work over the summer that the hotel connected to the theatre was haunted by a spirit. I had an apartment in the neighboring town, but sometimes I had to stay at the hotel where the performance had taken place. Often times a thick fog would settle in and make driving at night around the curvy mountain roads dangerous. Every time I had to sleep at that hotel I had horrible nightmares that I was being choked and would wake up to find nobody in the room but experienced a cold chill that kept me up for hours. While I never saw a ghost, I do believe the room had negative energy and my subconscious mind was experiencing the oppression as I slept. Other guests also reported having similar experiences and some even felt that they were being watched as they slept. My experience has led me to actually pray or say a blessing over the room before I go to bed. Some people have told me that if they ring a bell or leave a nightlight on, it changes the energy state of the room and provides for more restful sleep.

However, if you are excited about getting in contact with the unknowable force or energy it can be a great time to receive messages in your sleep from beyond this world. I would advise that you do not attempt to experiment in this area if you feel any unease because it can be very traumatic when the visitor is perceived as menacing. Nightmares are more prevalent in children than adults. In my opinion, the reason is because so many things are unknown to them and they are experiencing so many firsts in life. Without prior knowledge of how to handle some of these situations the child begins to have fears that manifest as night terrors. Also, children in general are more sensitive to emotional imbalances in the home or changes in positive and negative energies.

I also discovered that toddlers are unable dream about or see themselves in a dream until about the age of 4 or 5.

Lucid Dreaming is one of the most effect ways to eliminate nightmares. Once you have conscious control of the dream you can change the plot and bring help into the dream to bring about a feeling of confidence and positive resolution to the nightmare.

THE PROCESS OF INCUBATION

It is important to practice certain techniques to train the brain and program a lucid dream. My favorite technique is called ⋯

THE ART OF REVERSING

Tibetan monks have said that to do this practice for 7 years would equate to a lifetime of meditation and shorten the span for nirvana or enlightenment. I use this technique for reorganizing the fragmented images leftover from a dream remembered upon wakening to reverse an outcome of the problem. I also use the ART

OF REVERSING to identify my own bell words and mannerisms.

The Process: Start by imagining that you are sitting in a big comfortable chair in front of a movie screen. See in front of you a movie of your day playing out with you as the main character. There is one thing different than a typical movie scene, the movie reel is running in reverse order. So, you are seeing yourself going through your day from finish to start. This sharpens your brain and helps you to be more aware of when there is a message or synchronistic event in your waking daily life.

Using the Art of Reversal for Dream Programming

Here is an example:

Let's say I woke up and remembered I had a dream my sister was getting married. The only thing I could remember was something about live frogs jumping onto the wedding cake and a clown singing the Star Spangled Banner. I would take the main symbols - wedding, frogs, cake, clown, singing and patriotism writing them down quickly before forgetting. The next night as I lay down to sleep, I tell my brain what those symbols mean to me and reverse the problem by creating a beneficial outcome. I imagine a perfect wedding where the cake was beautiful and a very talented singer performed a very entertaining appropriate song. By pre-programming the conscious mind to reverse the dream, I will either create another dramatic response to oppose the message as I dream again or I will have my brain create a different scenario. This art of dream reversal can also be done if a person is interrupted during a dream sequence.

The important technique to remember is repetition of these exercises, forcing the subconscious to learn how to communicate with the conscious brain symbols so we can easily interpret them.

DREAM ANALYSIS

The problem with most dream analysis is that most resources seek universal interpretations for symbols that won't work most of the time. These are more advanced techniques and require the individual to learn about their unique sleep cycles and also to use a specific method each time they dream that can signal them to awake within the dream without waking up completely. Most of the time when we become aware we are dreaming it is difficult to stay in the dream.

To be more specific, I use conscious programming of hypnotic techniques. I am a certified hypno-therapist and have learned that we can control the subconscious mind with associations of powerful word triggers. It is important that a person define their own set of basic symbols and their meanings so we can use them as the signal for the subconscious mind to align with the conscious as we go into a dream state.

For example, if I define my symbols as such: Tree- growth, prosperity, and abundance Hawk- freedom, change, travel Water- forgiveness, new direction, healing Spider- deceit, unfaithful friend, complications, gossip House- family, happiness, stability, children.

I create my own meanings for about 15 to 30 symbols that represent answers to basic questions we seek. These are taken from my list of positive and negative neuro-associations I have collected into my dream notebook. Of course, the meanings are different for each person. Before going to sleep a person will mentally rehearse the dream using a guided script template inserting their key symbols and words every night to help the subconscious mind use recognize the pattern and become lucid.

HOW TO ANALYZE YOUR DREAM

Form vs. Content: Most people spend their time analyzing the content of the dream Unlike modern dream interpretation, Edgar Cayce known as the sleeping prophet- who was able to access knowledge in a deep trance like state, emphasizing that form was more important than content or symbols in a meaningful dream. Cayce claimed that in dreams people could receive valuable insight into their own lives, and that the insight was always of use to the dreamer.

Besides regular daily insight into one's life, he claimed people could communicate with loved ones (dead or alive), remember past life experiences, see a possible future and experience many other psychic abilities so long as the individual was ready to hear such knowledge and it was meant to help a person. Cayce claimed that everyone could experience this type of dreaming.

Dream Form - How is the Dream itself structured? Is it a moving dream? Is it third person? Is it vivid or ordinary? Black and White or Color? Is it compressed and disjointed or detailed and narrative in nature. Is it long or short? A Repetitive or a Dream Sequence? Past, Present or Future?

Dreams Always have 3 meanings:

1. Literal Interpretation

2. Emotional - identify the main emotion being conveyed or felt. Also, identify the immediate feeling and emotions after waking up from the dream.
3. Abstract Interpretation - look at any symbols or guides (central figures) to see if there are messages or metaphors based on your collection of personal nero-activators.

Always Identify the Form First! – (This is the most

important because it immediately identifies the nature of the dream.)

See precognition and dreams for more insight.

RECOGNIZING YOUR DREAM ARCHITECTURE

Are there any types of dreams you have consistently? For example, dreaming of work or a certain place like a school, park or particular time of day. Can you determine if there are certain themes you have over and over? Ex. Flying dreams or dreams where you are being chased, dreams where you are in nature. Jot down 3 places where you find yourself in a dream.

**According to a survey, the most common setting for dreams is your own house.

Examples of themes:

1. Plays - Performing in a Theatre
2. Dreams of Planes - flying and crashing
3. Weddings
4. Childhood friends and places from childhood.

RECOGNIZING YOUR DREAM GUIDE

Do you dream of certain people in your dream? Is there a consistent figure in your dream? How about an animal? People who have died?

It is helpful to identify your common characters in your dreams because they have special significance as your dream guides. Typically, these dream figures are trying to help you resolve issues or communicate a message.

How to find your ideal communication style: How do you communicate and receive information? (Pick two in which the description resonates with you)

Visual - You are able to memorize easily with reading, respond emotionally to colors, dream in color and have vivid imagination. You are attracted to appearance and speak to others in descriptive details.

Auditory - can easily memorize songs or lectures without taking notes, sometimes hear subtle sounds others do not hear. You hear sounds or realize that outside noises affected your dreams. You are attracted to others because of their voice quality and you are a lover of music. You need sound (listening to radio) in order to concentrate or study. People say you are a good listener.

Tactile - You learn by doing and probably enjoy hobbies like gardening or crafts. You are a touchy feely person when you talk and enjoy hugs. You are attracted to anything that appeals to your enjoyment of touch. You probably pick clothes that are more comfortable and quality material than looks. Your dreams are sensual in nature and you find that you are often participating not watching in your dreams.

Olfactory -You can easily recall a special memory, place or person if you associate the smell. Often times you are sensitive to certain odors and can be easily aroused or turned off by scent. Your dreams have a realistic touch because you can taste and smell in the moment.

The importance of knowing how you receive information will help you pick ways to communicate with your subconscious mind during the lucid dreaming. (I am very auditory so I always preprogram auditory triggers or have my guides playing an instrument because it stirs powerful emotions and makes the lucid experience last longer.)

**People that are blind from birth dream just as much as everyone else, however, their dreams are formed from their other senses such as touch, smell, taste and sound.*

PRECOGNITION AND LUCID DREAMING

The act of Dreaming on it! I am sure you are familiar with the old tradition of sleeping on a piece of wedding cake to dream of your future spouse? There are many examples of superstition involving putting things under your pillow to dream of the future. Today, we hear of dream pillows where silk pouches filled with lavender and other sleep inducing herbs can create a peaceful and positive dreaming experience. I have had people ask me if I recommend sleeping with crystals or other things like magnetic mattress pads and all natural sheet fibers.

Certain researchers who delve into lucid dreaming claim that these practices help raise the energy or vibrations that are connected to accessing the benefits of lucid dreams. I used to sleep with recorded information playing all night long to imbed the information into my subconscious mind. While, I do feel this can actually interfere with the ability to have significant dreaming experiences: the act of passive listening can cause the brain to soak up the information in a relaxed manner accelerating the learning curves of foreign language retention or memorization exercises for test preparation. I have also seen and experienced creative solutions and problem solving by just literally sleeping on it!

In college, music theory always was very difficult for me and the act of composing music sometimes clicked and other times was a tenuous experience to say the least. Many times before a project was due I would sleep on the recorded work and to my pleasant surprise I would either dream of a counter melody or a more advanced version of the song. Upon waking, the feeling I had was one of euphoria and excitement mixed with the fear that somehow the song was already composed by someone else. This fear was always replaced with awe as I realized the piece of music was indeed a new song composed from my mind! Because I was a vocal major, foreign language interpretation and diction was an important part of the singer's education. I found that I was always behind the learning curve in memorizing the languages. However, every time I used this method of listening to the language pronunciations I found that my dreams included me conversing or hearing the foreign language as part of a fluent process of communication. Upon waking I did not have instant command of the language as I understood it in the dream state but it boosted my confidence and always helped with the retaining of that information.

Precognition while dreaming is not as rare an occurrence as most would assume. The problem with studying and quantifying research in this area is that scientists cannot validate the existence of this reported phenomenon since most precognitive dreams lack exact data that tells of the time and place or 100% accuracy in the event. Also, precognitive dreams are not reported on a wide scale because most who have them only remember they have had the dream predicting the event as the event occurs.

The reason why this happens is that many precognitive dreams are conveyed in abstract form versus literal form. Also, many precognitive dreams are of mundane daily events and familiar people which do not strike a vivid enough impression to warrant writing the down the details. Instead, many sense feelings of déjà-vu or strange emotions from places and people not knowing that in previous dreams these places and people were already seen or revealed to them.

I have personally also had problems knowing when the precognitive dream applies in the future timeline of events. Sometimes, the dream occurs in a few days and at other times years later.

The theory of how precognition is achieved while dreaming is starting to be conceived or explained by resonance theories and new paradigms of time lacking linear direction. If one thinks of time as being circular with past, present and future existence occurring simultaneously, a person should be able to experience important events and access data regardless of location of distance or calendar date. The problem starts occurring with the belief system of whether future or past events are fixed or changeable.

I have always taken the belief system that certain events, which are important for mankind or the individual, are fixed but there are an infinite number of changeable circumstances that help create alternative outcomes from that event or series of past events. For example, let's say we know our great grandparents came over to Ellis Island and settled in Kentucky and then our grandfather died in a coal mine. Can we access information from the past to change that event? No because our knowledge of that event already makes it fixed and now our mind cannot perceive of it not happening. However, we can use lucid dreaming techniques to change certain perspectives of how that event negatively impacted us. Thereby, changing perhaps the present and future lessons. Think of life as one giant lesson with many assignments and death as the graduation day where we find out how we did and get to move on to a new existence. While this book is not going to delve into quantum physics or try to explain string theory, I will try exploring some ideas that might prove to be backed at some point by these new scientific areas of study.

Let's say I have a regret that I did not go in to the military when I was younger. One might say that if I did go into the military I would have never met my husband and then would not have moved to California or had my daughter, or gotten divorced, nor met my future husband. However, I believe that no matter my decision, all these other benefits would have still been given to me perhaps in another order or place and time. Upon meeting my second husband I found out that he had been accepted to a prestigious college in Berkeley, California.

He ended up choosing to go to a different college in another state. However, since he is four years younger than me, if I had chosen to go into the military I would have definitely been stationed in Fort Myers. My theory is that he would have chosen to go to college in Berkeley and we would have inevitably met which might have been earlier in the timeline of the actual past.

So what would that mean if it had happened that way? Well, instead of staying married to my first husband five years and having a ten year period before getting married again; this change, may have caused me to get divorced earlier and could have allowed me to get married again way before 2008. A myriad of things would have changed for me but somehow I believe we would have ended up in Oregon. This move may have occurred when I retired from the military or perhaps moving earlier due to his parents living out there in southern Oregon. Either way, I would probably have encountered some of the same people in my life currently and perhaps have had some of the same experiences. So, my belief is that there are infinite paths to get to the same chosen events that are meant for us to experience and people to connect with in our lifetime.

By knowing how to lucid dream, we can literally help ourselves take the best path to our happiest experiences and find our ultimate destiny faster. Now, most of you are probably saying to yourself, " what if I don't choose to believe this about time or about how destiny or lack of destiny works?"

Well, that is ok because regardless of your beliefs about how it all works, the benefits of accessing this information will be something you can do nightly and directs your perspective accordingly to the information you obtain.

Precognitive dreams can help us prepare emotionally and mentally for those dramatic life transforming moments when we hear bad news or have an event that brings personal trauma. My instruction stems from the premise that if you change the precognition during the dream you can change the future to bring the most beneficial conclusion from that event. I don't teach that you can change the actual event itself.

While that may be a philosophy many have and strive to achieve while lucid dreaming, I focus more on creating a healthy response and turning any negative event to show the positive healing aspects faster for the person in the waking life.

Think about those past events in your life that you wished you had prior knowledge of to change it from happening. Now, most of us can look at prior traumas and events as ways to bring about positive change in our lives. For example, often times in looking at my past I can see how these negative events were actually positive agents of change to bring something even more wonderful and beneficial to my life. Yes, even if it involves loss and pain.

The hard part of going through these difficult trials is the actual time it takes to bring about the healing and new changes that will usher in another opportunity. How nice would it be to have prior knowledge that when you get fired from your job 6 months from now you can have peace to accept that it is a good thing for you because a more fulfilling job is coming with better pay and benefits 9 months from now. So, you won't change the event from happening but you will have a whole new perspective about it prior to having the emotional pain of loss.

While you have probably had a precognitive dream or known of someone who has experienced one, the problem of pinpointing the timing and other details can make the whole sharing of the event frustrating. Without a specific target for creating a precognitive dream we are left aimless sorting through endless possibilities of how and when the event are going to transpire. For example, many people dreamed of 911 before the event, myself included. However, most of those dreams were interpreted and realized as a prophetic dream after the event took place.

The majority of dreams were just too abstract to see and connect the dots of the event. Also, in many cases those that did tell someone of the dream did not receive validation of those fears or warnings.

So does that mean we just don't tell anyone because it will go unheeded? Should we just disregard these dreams because by the time we figure it out it will be too late to do any good? I have had these thoughts many times and while I think that some events cannot be stopped from happening I have figured a way to clarify and analyze them with more accuracy.

The first step is to narrow down the playing field of possible targets so our mind can choose to reveal to us only the future concerns that directly impact our life and those we love.

So, before you attempt to dream of the future, make a list of those topics you most would like to have insight and knowledge. I would suggest starting with your own life, rather than world events or solving crimes of the latest America's most Wanted. While these are noble pursuits, you will have more success in starting with your own personal pool of people and self.

Write down your question before going to sleep.

As you are drifting into the "grog state" let the question come into your mind and be confident that you will receive your answers. Use two or three symbols from your collected list so you will recognize them as affirmation that this is indeed a future message meant for you. The symbols should be pictured visually and used as part of your template. The first few times of attempting this technique can be frustrating and you will probably have trouble matching any dreams with an obvious answer to your questions.

However, if you just keep practicing this method along using one of the specific templates and memory retrieval tools, you will start seeing success in your waking life. Typically it takes the mind a consecutive focused attempt for 14-18 days to make this breakthrough. As this happens, you will need to pay attention to how the dream was presented to you.

Many precognitive dreams accompany a different feel from regular dreams and each person experiences them uniquely. For example, you may find that usually you dream in color and your precognitive dreams are in black and white without sound. Or, every precognitive dream is accompanied by a specific sound or feeling. One person reported that they feel the hair rising on the back of their neck when they are having a dream about the future. Others report hearing a high buzzing sound or even speaking telepathically in their dreams.

I typically am a watcher experiencing a change to 3rd person and many of my precognitive dreams also have my childhood dream guide appear with a message. Some will have the message delivered to them by departed relatives or animals and others will have the dream accompanied by a specific aroma they smell upon waking or during the dream itself.

After a while, you can be more confident in knowing which of your dreams is an actual precognition dream. If you still are not sure if a dream of yours is a future dream event, you can ask the same question the next night and record any further dreams that validate the authenticity of the message or discredit the dream. Usually, the dream will occur again the next night or have aspects and characters that affirm it is part of the same message. If the question is asked again and you dream of completely random non-relating themes; than it would probably not be a precognitive dream. However, keep repeating the question for several nights just to affirm that there was not a delay in delivering the confirmation.

The most commonly reported precognitive dream is in the form of a nightmare. It is presented in a negative form to grab our conscious attention and wake us to feel the impact of the emotions so we will remember the warning or message. However, don't think that just because you have a bad dream it is prophetic. I used to make this mistake because so many nightmares seem so powerful and real. The accompaniment of super charged emotions and reactions upon waking make it so tempting to think these dreams must be precognizant.

OBE - OUT OF BODY EXPERIENCES

One of the most sought after experience in Lucid Dreaming is the ability to travel outside the body in an astral vehicle to experience the future and access higher knowledge. This experience is called Astral Projection and is different from Lucid Dreaming.

Children seem to have the ability to astral project more effortlessly than adults. One possibility is because children are more open to the possibility and do not have limiting beliefs or preconceived fears about leaving their bodies. Astral Projection should not

be attempted until you have successfully experienced
Lucidity in your dreams on a regular basis.

The process of astral travel while dreaming can be
dangerous and without prior steps to insure your
safety the first experience could be a negative one. I
do believe that astral dream travel is one of the most
effective ways to access the future and problem solve.
I have used astral travel to remote view lost objects
and gain valuable information. You can literally travel
anywhere in the world or universe and come back to
your sleeping body with a wealth of knowledge and
spiritual enlightenment.

Remember, that the lucid dream state can create
solutions in your waking life through meaningful
coincidences and events. Often times, the beginner will
find it frustrating to achieve lucidity unless there is
consistent effort in practicing these techniques. Don't
give up too easily because the act of programming a
dream alone can bring about so many beneficial
outcomes.
I also recommend using the Lucid Dreaming hypnosis
CD I have created to help relax you into the ideal
brainwave state needed to access the subconscious
mind.

SUMMARY OF GUIDE: <u>Form VS. Content:</u>

1. Literal or Abstract in Nature

2. Color and vivid or dull and boring-B/W

3. Movement and Action or Watching 3rd person

4. Central Characters or Subject Matter

5. Detailed Narrative or Condensed and disjointed.

6. Repetitive or Dream Sequence

LUCID COMMANDS

1. Start practicing in the "grog state" first. Use the art of reversing to lower your brainwave state into relaxation.

2. Picture yourself in your dream architecture as you are walking through your template repeat your affirmations of conscious awareness telling yourself

that tonight you will remember to test your reality while you sleep.

3. Have a specific goal for your dream. Tell yourself you will receive an answer or the insight you are seeking.

4. Try to remain conscious until the very last second repeating opening and closing the eyes or staring at a dot in the ceiling etc.

5. As you dream, if there is a momentary thought of this is odd⋯take immediate action! Try spinning or asking a question-movement and focus can keep lucidity from fading.

7. Perform your lucid "act" of oddness to test your reality or state your questions immediately. Ex. (try spinning around, flying or reading something more than once) stay calm because if you get too excited you will wake up.

6. Practice the same routine each night to train your brain before you attempt a different dream template.

8. Keep dream journal - consistently try to jot down the form and basic 3 meanings of dream. Match any positive or negative neuro-associations that you remember to your list.

1. Experiment with finding your ideal "sleep cycle."

2. During the day test your reality often and become aware of any synchronistic events or déjà-vu feelings. Notice what and who commands your attention and focus. Continue to add these associations to your dream journal.

Precognition

1. Narrow down your field of focus. Set an intention that provokes strong emotions and personally involve your daily relationships and activities or environment.

2. During the day pay special attention to any little intuitive moments you notice. (ex. Predicting the phone ringing or knowing what someone was going to say as they spoke.)

3. Write down in your journal any physical triggers or emotional triggers before the "psi" event. (ex. Nauseas feeling, goose bumps, ringing in the ear, smell, seeing a color or hearing a voice.)

4. Always set up your dream template with your symbolic anchors to confirm your questions and provide you insight into the dream's meaning.

5. Use the specific dream template that targets the subject of answers you are seeking.

6. Identify any dream guides, or clues that point to a precognitive dream. Ex. 3rd person, especially unique compared to other dreams, strong feelings, telepathic communication, unusual sounds or smells, seeing relatives or friends in the dream who have died.

7. Look for repetitive or dream sequences to confirm or negate the message within two weeks of the dream.

8. Take "action" upon waking in your daily life or in your next lucid dream.

9. Look for your dream symbols during the day as confirmation of previous dream messages.

DREAM TEMPLATES

#1 - The Treasure Hunt: Dream Architecture for Success or Abundance

Allow your mind to remember a place outdoors that you associate with positive feelings and experiences. It can be a childhood playground or a favorite camping spot. One of my favorite places is a pile of rocks I used to climb up in Colorado to see a spectacular view. It can even be a picture from a magazine like a secluded island or cave. As you imagine this place see the details and look for a map. You will find it somewhere in this place. This map will provide you with clues as to solving your greatest issue. If you are having troubles with reading the map its ok just imagine that it has the information you need and be confident you will solve your problem. Now take the map with you and let your mind start focusing on certain symbols you are sure to find on your way. You can keep looking in the same area or step out of this happy place. Make sure you are feeling those emotions of happiness, security, and warmth whatever it is that brings a smile as you drift off to sleep. Look for the symbols that signify your success.

These symbols could be, a green tree, a deer, a pot of gold or an agate rock or a serene waterfall? If you are having trouble finding any of these symbols its ok just keep walking and see in your mind anything that creates an impression on you. Now take the map and unroll it again and imagine that you can see a big x somewhere on the map. It signifies the answer to your question or the solution. As you look at the map can you see anything else? Its okay if you feel like you are making it up as you look at the map. Remember, your subconscious mind already knows the answer to your question so even if you feel like you are just creating your dream; the probability is that your subconscious mind is influencing your thoughts and directing you.

Place: choose location of treasure hunt.

Symbols: select 3 symbols of abundance or success.

Guide: choose person or animal you will be encountering for messages or target questions.

Sensory clue: pick a sound, feeling, or color you will be able to easily focus on during incubation period and in dream state.

Question: (open ended with clear intent) only one question per dream in the beginning until more consistent.

Action: what movement are you going to do once you acknowledge conscious awareness?

#2 - The Hearth and Home Dream Architecture for Love, Friendship, Family and Relationships

We are going to start by imagining a home. This can be your dream home or a childhood home from your past. It can also be another home that you loved, like grandparents or friends. Just make sure it is a home that you experienced love and happy times. A home can be a castle, a log cabin, a tree house, or even an old home. First create how many rooms there will be and you will label each one with a theme. The kitchen represents your mother or any other female, like a sister or in law. Children are going to be represented by a playroom or the recreation room. The bedroom is always your spouse or lover. The garage represents areas that we need to clean out and get rid of in our lives. The living room represents friends and the library or den; office represents our father, and males in our lives. The closets represent hidden things that you don't know about. The bathroom denotes health issues or areas we need to pay extra attention for healing!!

In your template of your home you are going to place positive associations in each room. These will be selected from your dictionary of symbols. As an example, in the kitchen, you are going to place flowers or a favorite painting.

The bedroom you will have it be your favorite color and see a special clock or beautiful lamp. Any symbol you equate with love would be appropriate to place in that room. In the bathroom, you are going to have a symbol denoting health, which might be a green plant or a little water fountain on the counter. You could place a beautiful comfy robe on the back of the door. Go through each room and place 2 or 3 special symbols. This might take some time, but at night or before you go to bed, repeat the affirmation that you will dream of this house and see your symbols in each of the rooms to trigger lucidity and familiarity. Once you have recognition immediately take action or ask a specific question-figure out ahead of time what that action will be. For example you might say to yourself "who is going to visit me soon? " who in this house is going to leave soon?"

(indicates separation or even death) this is especially true if you see this person coming out of the bathroom. Remember to keep it simple with only one question per lucid dream.

Place: pick your ideal house-you can get detailed but in the beginning make it simple.

Symbols: choose from your list of positive neuro associations and place 1-3 symbols per room in house.

Guide: focus on a person or animal you will see when you are dreaming and affirm that this guide will have a gift or message for you.

Sensory clue: pick a sound, feeling, or color you will be able to easily focus on during incubation period and in dream state.

Question: make sure it relates to relationships or home concerns

Action: decide what action you are going to take upon lucidity.

#3 The Temple: For spiritual guidance, higher knowledge, creative projects and inspiration. Use the Temple for Remote Viewing targets.

Place yourself in front of a beautiful sanctuary. This sanctuary can be an old stone church or a place in the woods. You can make it a cathedral or a floating glass modern temple on a cloud. Next, you are going to create for yourself a guide that you will meet at the temple. This might be in the form of a bird or your favorite animal; it could be a person that you find wise. You can imagine the guide as jesus or another religious figure but this template should resonate with your personal spiritual beliefs. If you don't have spiritual beliefs you can make it a science laboratory or a guide who looks like einstein. As you find this temple you should see yourself standing outside and hearing beautiful music-pick a song that you will recognize. Then you will go inside the doors and find a huge stone alter or lab table with gifts for you to examine. My dream alter would always be piled high with scrolls that were tied with red velvet ribbon and sometimes there would be an elaborate looking book encrusted with jewels. When i try to open the book it usually becomes a portal taking me somewhere else.

Place: choose a temple, church or place of higher learning.

Symbols: pick 2 or 3 symbols that represent knowledge or spiritual guidance. Place these symbols near or on your alter so you will recognize them.

Guide: whom do you know that is a spiritual mentor or someone that represents the faith that you practice? (you can even choose st. Theresa, gandhi, jesus or even a local pastor that you trust. You can also choose an animal instead.

Sensory clue: is there incense burning on the alter? Is there angels singing or chanting? Pick your sound, smell or color that will enhance your lucidity. Lots of people think the color blue represents spirituality or white.

Question: what higher knowledge are you seeking? Ask with a preface of knowing for my highest good and for the good of others. (some knowledge isn't meant for us to know.)

Action: decide the specific action you are going to take upon achieving lucidity.

Template #4 -The Tree-for questions concerning the body/health and wellness

Imagine the tree represents your body. Pick a tree you resonate with on a personal level. In your dream architecture, imagine you see this tree as solitary and in a setting that you can easily distinguish and recognize it when you enter the lucid state. My special tree was always the "juicy fruit" gum tree from a commercial i saw growing up. I always recognized it because it had gum growing off it instead of fruit. You could place the tree in a special garden or by a river or in a field. As you look at the tree be as observant as possible. The trunk represents your core body and the roots your feet. The branches your arms and the top your neck and head. The leaves represent your skin and the fruit or whatever is growing off of it like hazelnuts represent the state of your health. While you are in a lucid dream look at your tree to notice the changes. If there is lots of fruit you are healthy and vibrant. Is the tree losing its leaves? Is it covered in moss? Is it colorful with red and orange leaves? Does it have flowers? If your tree has flowers and smells delicious it represents the natural beauty and charisma you have that attracts people to you. Is it covered with frost or snow? The seasons can also point to certain times to pay attention to your health. For example···be extra cautious in winter because you may slip on the ice and break your leg. As you practice this template you will be able to interpret your own meanings especially as you place special symbols in or around your tree to help clarify and trigger lucidity.

Place: pick a type of tree and location of that tree. (be detailed)

Symbols: choose two or three symbols that represent health, fertility or wellness and place those in or around your tree. (for example) i place my tree next to a waterfall, which represents to me energy and strength. You could have your tree have jewels with diamonds and emeralds hanging off the branches to denote beauty and attraction. Get creative!!

Guide: select a person or animal that you will encounter each time you practice and enter the dream architecture of the tree! Ex. You could have an elf or fairy in the tree, a bird you talk to or a squirrel or wise owl.

Sensory clue: decide the season of your tree template. Is it fall, spring or summer? Are you hot, cold or warm? How does your tree smell? Does the tree smell woodsy, pine or floral, fruity or just fresh? Choose music that you will hear when you see your tree. (i like my guide to be playing the flute when i see my tree.)

Question: what is your deepest concern for your health or the health of someone you know? You can ask questions concerning your mental wellbeing or any athletic endeavors work well for this template too.

Action: decide what movement you are going to do upon knowledge of lucidity.

Tools and Resources For Further Study of Lucid Dreaming!

Books:

"The History Of Dreams," Robert Moss
"Lucid Fiction" Short Stories by 7 Authors
"The Art Of Lucid Dreaming" by Rebecca Turner
"Dreaming An Introduction to The Science Of Sleep" by J, Allen Hobson.
"Exploring The World Of Lucid Dreaming" by Stephen Laberge

Websites:

www.instituteofluciddreaming.com

www.the-world-of-lucid-dreaming.com
www.theacadamyofdreams.com
www.lucidity.com
www.astrozone.com

Hypnosis and NLP:

www.apositiva.com

Electronics:

Iphone app: "sleep cycle" gemini light and sound machine: helps lower brain wave state for relaxation.

Dream masks:

Flashing light helps wake you during rem. CD's: Hemisync, Kelly Howell, Centerpointe

DVD

"Waking Life," "Vanilla Sky," "Lucid Dreaming Series" By Hemisync

Essential oils: rose essential oil for lucid dreaming-the best! Earth solutions aromatherapy scent inhaler (lucid dreaming scent) herbs and supplements: mugwort for memory-wrapped in cloth under pillow.

Rocks and gems:

Quartz crystals-known to hold recorded information" many dreamers focus on their problems and actually sleep on the crystal" (my favorite) amethyst for dream recall: azurite for accessing intuition through dreams lepidolite for nightmares and insomnia: moldavite for advanced dream work: - (I like this stone for OBE experiences) helps for higher lucidity.

Remote viewing:

For fun you can try to remote view the front page of the newspaper. At first you will just get the themes not the headlines because it is difficult to retain written information upon waking.

Another fun exercise is to remote view a friend. I like to practice this one while i am taking a nap in the middle of the day. This only works if there is a strong connection between the two of you. So don't get discouraged if you can't remote view your neighbor or your grocery store clerk. I used to ask my husband if he enjoyed lunch out on certain days and he seriously thought i was stalking him!

Lost objects:

We have all wanted to find something we have lost. Remote viewing works well for objects that stir a strong sentimental attachment. Try pre-programming your lucid dream to locate your lost object by picturing that you can communicate with the object itself! Use the treasure hunt dream template to have the map lead you to the object. Don't worry if you wake up and the map didn't seem to point out the object directly. Remember that it will probably be abstract or symbolic. The more practice will help you understand the clues. If after two weeks you do not get a psychic knowing than the object is permanently gone and unable to be retrieved.

ABOUT THE AUTHOR

Patricia Smith, MA became interested in dreams due to a childhood struggle with nightmares that increased during her teens. After trying to find an explanation ranging from chemical imbalances, too much sugar, repressed trauma, and even the possibility of demons!

She discovered Dr. Stephen Laberge who was particularly interested in a unique type of dreaming experience called Lucid Dreaming, a type of dream had many reported benefits including overcoming nightmares.

Patricia continues to research lucid dreaming and other altered states of consciousness.

www.ingramcontent.com/pod-product-compliance
Lightning Source LLC
Chambersburg PA
CBHW071638050426
42443CB00026B/711